Politician

CAREERS WITH CHARACTER

CAREERS WITH CHARACTER

Politician

Ellyn Sanna

Mason Crest

Mason Crest
450 Parkway Drive, Suite D
Broomall, PA 19008
www.masoncrest.com

Printed in the Hashemite Kingdom of Jordan.

First printing
9 8 7 6 5 4 3 2 1

Series ISBN: 978-1-4222-2750-3
ISBN: 978-1-4222-2762-6
ebook ISBN: 978-1-4222-9058-3

The Library of Congress has cataloged the
hardcopy format(s) as follows:

Library of Congress Cataloging-in-Publication Data

Sanna, Ellyn, 1957-
  Politician / Ellyn Sanna.
     pages cm. – (Careers with characters)
  Includes index.
     ISBN 978-1-4222-2762-6 (hardcover) – ISBN 978-1-4222-2750-3 (series) – ISBN 978-1-4222-9058-3 (ebook)
  1. Politics, Practical–Vocational guidance–United States–Juvenile literature. 2. Politicians–United States–Juvenile literature. I. Title.
  JK1726.S323 2014
  324.023'73–dc23
                              2013007512

Produced by Vestal Creative Services.
www.vestalcreative.com

Photo Credits:
Alanpoulson | Dreamstime.com: p. 55
Comstock: p. 88
Corbis: pp. 20, 28, 36, 40, 41, 44, 58, 62, 65, 66
Dover, Dictionary of American Portraits: pp. 25, 46, 47, 48
PhotoDisc: pp. 14, 15, 22, 30, 31, 32, 33, 59, 64, 69, 72, 74, 76, 77, 79, 81, 84, 85, 86
PhotoSpin: pp. 17, 23, 24, 38, 67

The individuals in these images are models, and the images are for illustrative purposes only. To the best knowledge of the publisher, all other images are in the public domain. If any image has been inadvertently uncredited or miscredited, please notify Vestal Creative Services, Vestal, New York 13850, so that rectification can be made for future printings.

CONTENTS

We each leave a fingerprint on the world.
Our careers are the work we do in life.
Our characters are shaped by the choices
we make to do good.
When we combine careers with character,
we touch the world with power.

INTRODUCTION

by Dr. Cheryl Gholar
and Dr. Ernestine G. Riggs

In today's world, the awesome task of choosing or staying in a career has become more involved than one would ever have imagined in past decades. Whether the job market is robust or the demand for workers is sluggish, the need for top-performing employees with good character remains a priority on most employers' lists of "must have" or "must keep." When critical decisions are being made regarding a company or organization's growth or future, job performance and work ethic are often the determining factors as to who will remain employed and who will not.

How does one achieve success in one's career and in life? Victor Frankl, the Austrian psychologist, summarized the concept of success in the preface to his book *Man's Search for Meaning* as: "The unintended side-effect of one's personal dedication to a course greater than oneself." Achieving value by responding to life and careers from higher levels of knowing and being is a specific goal of teaching and learning in "Careers with Character." What constitutes success for us as individuals can be found deep within our belief system. Seeking, preparing, and attaining an excellent career that aligns with our personality is an outstanding goal. However, an excellent career augmented by exemplary character is a visible expression of the human need to bring meaning, purpose, and value to our work.

Career education informs us of employment opportunities, occupational outlooks, earnings, and preparation needed to perform certain tasks. Character education provides insight into how a person of good character might choose to respond, initiate an action, or perform specific tasks in the presence of an ethical dilemma. "Careers with Character" combines the two and teaches students that careers are more than just jobs. Career development is incomplete without character development. What better way to explore careers and character than to make them a single package to be opened, examined, and reflected upon as a means of understanding the greater whole of who we are and what work can mean when one chooses to become an employee of character?

Character can be defined simply as "who you are even when no one else is around." Your character is revealed by your choices and actions. These bear your personal signature, validating the story of who you are. They are the fingerprints you leave behind on the people you meet and know; they are the ideas you bring into reality. Your choices tell the world what you truly believe.

Character, when viewed as a standard of excellence, reminds us to ask ourselves when choosing a career: "Why this particular career, for what purpose, and to what end?" The authors of "Careers with Character" knowledgeably and passionately, through their various vignettes, enable one to experience an inner journey that is both intellectual and moral. Students will find themselves, when confronting decisions in real life, more prepared, having had experiential learning opportunities through this series. The books, however, do not separate or negate the individual good from the academic skills or intellect needed to perform the required tasks that lead to productive career development and personal fulfillment.

Each book is replete with exemplary role models, practical strategies, instructional tools, and applications. In each volume, individuals of character work toward ethical leadership, learning how to respond appropriately to issues of not only right versus wrong, but issues of right versus right, understanding the possible benefits and consequences of their decisions. A wealth of examples is provided.

What is it about a career that moves our hearts and minds toward fulfilling a dream? It is our character. The truest approach to finding out who we are and what illuminates our lives is to look within. At the very heart of career development is good character. At the heart of good character is an individual who knows and loves the good, and seeks to share the good with others. By exploring careers and character together, we create internal and external environments that support and enhance each other, challenging students to lead conscious lives of personal quality and true richness every day.

Is there a difference between doing the right thing, and doing things right? Career questions ask, "What do you know about a specific career?" Character questions ask, "Now that you know about a specific career, what will you choose to do with what you know?" "How will you perform certain tasks and services for others, even when no one else is around?" "Will all individuals be given your best regardless of their socioeconomic background, physical condition, ethnicity, or religious beliefs?" Character questions often challenge the authenticity of what we say we believe and value in the workplace and in our personal lives.

Character and career questions together challenge us to pay attention to our lives and not fall asleep on the job. Career knowledge, self-knowledge, and ethical wisdom help us answer deeper questions about the meaning of work; they give us permission to transform our lives. Personal integrity is the price of admission.

The insight of one "ordinary" individual can make a difference in the world—if that one individual believes that character is an amazing gift to uncap knowledge and talents to empower the human community. Our world needs everyday heroes in the workplace—and "Careers with Character" challenges students to become those heroes.

Abraham Lincoln's life as a politician demonstrated the need for learning, experience, and character.

JOB REQUIREMENTS

Education, experience, reputation ...
all of these are important requirements
for a career in politics.

CHAPTER ONE

Almost 200 years ago, a young boy grew up in the wilds of central United States. By the time he reached adulthood, he could read, write, and do arithmetic, but that was the extent of his education. He had little if any formal training for the life that lay ahead of him. But this young man was determined he would make a difference to his country.

He got a job as a farmhand; he split rails for fences; he was a storekeeper . . . and all the while, he worked hard to educate himself. Eventually, he became a captain who served in the Black Hawk War, and from there he went on to spend eight years serving in the Illinois legislature. He was also a judge who rode the *circuits* for many years. His law partner said of him, "His ambition was a little engine that knew no rest."

Because of this driving ambition, Abraham Lincoln went on to become President of the United States. During his years in office, he built the Republican Party into a strong national organization— and he reached across party lines, rallying most of the northern Democrats to the Union cause. On January 1, 1863, he issued the Emancipation Proclamation, freeing the slaves within the *Confederacy*.

This backwoods boy did more than he had ever dreamed. He never let the world forget that the Civil War involved an even larger issue than states' rights, as he stated in the speech he gave at the dedication of Gettysburg's military cemetery: "that we here highly

In Lincoln's day, a politician's success was built more on character than image.

resolve that these dead shall not have died in vain—that this nation, under God, shall have a new birth of freedom—and that government of the people, by the people, for the people, shall not perish from the earth." Lincoln's words and actions continue to influence today's America.

If Abraham Lincoln were alive today, however, he might not be the successful politician he was in his own time. Few if any political candidates today are self-educated, and many have impressive law degrees. Like Lincoln, today's politicians need to be powerful speakers who can influence people with their words—but they need to be able to do so in front of cameras, where millions of people around the world can hear and watch them. What's more, politicians in today's world need to be able to use the *media* as the primary focus of their *campaigns*. No longer is it enough to simply possess a reputation for wisdom and honesty, as Lincoln did. Public opinion of politicians depends now on their ability to project an image through the media. A poor boy from the country could

The Constitution of the United States, ratified by the last of the 13 original states in 1791, created three branches of the federal government and granted certain powers and responsibilities to each:

1. legislative (which makes the laws)
2. executive (enforces the laws)
3. judicial (the courts which interpret the laws)

This three-branched system was designed to keep politicians' power in balance.

About 89,000 local governments exist in the United States. These include about 3,000 county governments, 19,500 municipal governments, 16,400 townships, and 37,300 special districts. Illinois has the most local government unites, with more than 6,900, while Hawaii has the fewest, with only 21.

Taken from U.S. Bureau of the Census information.

Many politicians begin their careers as lawyers.

Ethical dilemmas take place whenever a person has to make a decision about right and wrong. Here's how author Richard N. Bolles describes these experiences:

There are dozens of such moments every day. Moments when you stand—as it were—at a . . . crossroads, with two ways lying before you. Such moments are typically called "moments of decision." It does not matter what the frame or content of each particular decision is. It all devolves, in the end, into just two roads before you, every time. The one will lead to less gratitude, less kindness, less forgiveness, less honesty, or less love in the world. The other will lead to more gratitude, more kindness, more forgiveness, more honesty, or more love in the world.

From *How to Find Your Mission in Life* by Richard Nelson Bolles (Berkeley, Calif.: Ten Speed Press, 2000), pp. 38–39.

never hope to compete, not without lots of education and training—and not without money.

Some things haven't changed since Lincoln's day, however. For instance, politicians today still have great power to do good in our world. They can still make a tremendous difference to their nation.

When the founders of the United States gathered in Philadelphia more than 200 years ago, they laid the foundations for self-governance in America. This means that the United States is not ruled by a king or a queen, nor by any other form of absolute government. Instead, American citizens elect their leaders—politicians who both lead and serve the public. Politicians can be elected to office at the federal, state, or local level.

The levels of government at which politicians hope to serve determine the qualifications those individuals need. The more impor-

A politician may work his way up from lawyer to judge to a higher local executive position.

16

Television (and radio) has changed politics. If you hope to win an election outside of local government, you need to buy time on television—and TV time is expensive. This means that candidates for major political offices have little chance of winning if they don't have money.

Some candidates are privately wealthy, but most have to seek support from rich and powerful companies and individuals. These people who fund candidates expect a payback in return. As a result, the opinions of the rich and powerful often influence politicians more than the views of ordinary citizens. Campaign finance reform has become an issue that needs to be addressed within the U.S. government.

tant and powerful the position, the more visible that position will be—and the more will be required of candidates. For instance, the chief executive of a small town or county may work less than 20 hours a week, and he or she may be an ordinary businessperson with far less legal training than Abraham Lincoln had. However, the education and background of candidates for state governor are scrutinized by the public far more closely—and the expectations for presidential candidates are still more demanding.

Training and educational requirements vary for political jobs. Like most professional jobs in any career sector, at least a four-year college degree is usually required. Most federal departments or agencies determine their own requirements for each position (including, in some cases, a minimum age). The education and experience

The Democratic National Committee (www.democrats.org) and the Republican National Committee (www.gop.com) offer candidate training that includes how-to materials and workshops; they also offer planning and consulting services to help candidates develop campaign strategies.

Communication Skills a Must

Before the 1994 election, Newt Gingrich, the Republicans' leader, sent out a memo to his party's candidates that was titled "Language: A Key Mechanism to Control." In the memo, his organization recommended that candidates use words like these:

share	opportunity	legacy	challenge	truth
change	moral	courage	prosperity	humane
liberty	caring	tough	help	dream
freedom	peace	rights	children	confident
initiative	passionate	protect	fair	preserve

The Republicans experienced a landslide victory in 1994 . . . perhaps in part because of their powerful use of words.

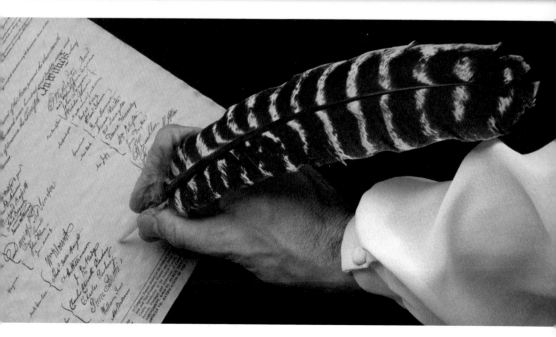

North America's earliest politicians helped shape today's government.

18

Not all politicians have degrees in law. Some becoming outstanding in another professional field and then move from there to politics. Alexa McDonough is the first woman to lead a major political party in Canada. She lead the New Democratic Party from 1995 to 2003, though she earned a degree in social work and worked for Social Services before entering government. Although Ms. McDonough might no longer be considered a social worker, she is still working to make things better for her fellow citizens—and as a politician, she has the political power to bring about change in her society.

needed for state and local politicians also vary. Most positions require a minimum age, as well as residency and citizenship.

Many politicians have backgrounds in law or political science. A master's degree in public administration is recommended (although not usually required) for city managers, as well as some other local government positions. Sometimes, however, politicians can work their way up through various positions, gaining experience and reputation as they go. For local executives and legislators, public support is usually the most important factor. Volunteer work and community services are good ways to gain a positive reputation.

When it comes to electing their leaders, the public has begun to look particularly closely at character issues. Tom Lickona, a character education expert, writes that good character depends on possessing certain core character qualities—like integrity, justice, and compassion. Values like these, says Lickona, are the traits that affirm our dignity as human beings. Living out these values is not only good for us as individuals; it is also good for the entire world. It creates a better place for us all to live.

Even a hint of past scandal can sometimes destroy a candidate's chances of election. Politicians live their lives in the public eye—and failures of character are hard to hide. In today's world, if you hope to be a successful politician, you must possess money and *charisma*, education and political *savvy*. But even more important, you must somehow balance all these other factors with the qualities of a good character:

- integrity and trustworthiness;
- respect and compassion;
- justice and fairness;
- responsibility;
- courage;
- self-discipline and diligence;
- citizenship.

As politicians struggle with these core character traits, they encounter countless ethical dilemmas. In the chapters that follow, we will examine how politicians face this challenge.

In every community there is work to be done. In every nation, there are wounds to heal. In every heart, there is the power to do it.

—Marianne Williamson

A politician may set out to be a trustworthy leader—but events often challenge his integrity.

INTEGRITY AND TRUSTWORTHINESS

Integrity means we practice what we preach.

CHAPTER TWO

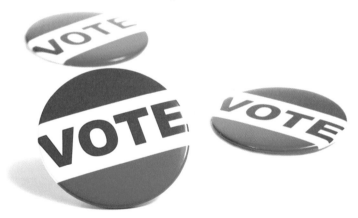

Mike Jefferson had set out to be an honest leader of his community. As an African American, he was eager to do all he could to help others who came from backgrounds similar to his. He believed passionately that African American boys needed strong male role models from within the black community, and he had plenty of good ideas for making that happen in his small Southern town. That was just one of Mike's ideas; he also wanted to tackle some of the school's problems as well as develop a training program for young adults who had dropped out of school. With so much he wanted to accomplish, running for mayor seemed like the logical thing to do. He knew he could be an honest and trustworthy

A politician must weigh the relative importance of issues. What do you think: How important is pollution compared to other community issues?

leader. So he was disappointed when he began to realize that his chances of being elected were slim. Other candidates had far more experience than he did.

Then one morning, just as Mike was opening his office door at the car dealership he owned, a man called out to him from across the parking lot. Mike recognized the owner of the local paper factory and invited him to come into his office.

The man had a proposition for Mike. The factory owner would see to it that Mike was elected mayor—and in return, Mike would close his eyes to the illegal waste products the factory was dumping into the river. "You've got good ideas, Mike," the factory owner finished. "I can help you make them happen. And all you need to do is help me out a little in return."

Mike had never thought much about environmental issues. They didn't seem as important to him as the plight of his community's children and young people. No one would ever know if he gave the factory owner what he wanted. But could Mike be a leader of

People who value integrity and trustworthiness:

- tell the truth.
- don't withhold important information.
- are sincere; they don't deceive, mislead, or be devious and tricky.
- don't betray a trust.
- don't steal.
- don't cheat.
- stand up for beliefs about right and wrong.
- keep their promises.
- return what they have borrowed and pay their debts.
- stand by, support, and protect their families, friends, community, and country.
- don't talk behind people's backs or spread rumors.
- don't ask their friends to do something wrong.

Adapted from material from the Character Counts Coalition, charactercounts.org/overview/about.html

George Washington, American's first president, had a reputation for honesty.

Presidents of the United States, like all human beings, must struggle with issues of integrity.

> When tempted to do anything in secret, ask yourself if you would do it in public; if you would not do it, be sure it is wrong.
> —Thomas Jefferson

integrity in those vital areas that mattered so much to him, if he let down his moral standards in other areas? Mike was not the first politician to struggle with this same issue.

Richard Nixon had been a smart, serious politician with plenty of ambition. When he became President, he worked hard to bring peace and prosperity to his nation. Unfortunately, at the same time he allowed his Republican staff to play illegal tricks on his Democratic opponents. They broke into the Democrat Party's headquarters (in the Watergate Hotel) and stole documents; they tapped phone lines and listened to private conversations; they told lies; and they used the government tax office to hurt Nixon's enemies. Then they paid "hush" money to keep people quiet so the truth would not become

The four enemies of integrity:

- self-interest (The things we want ... the things we might be tempted to lie, steal, or cheat to get.)
- self-protection (The things we don't want ... the things we'd lie, steal, or cheat to avoid.)
- self-deception (When we refuse to see the situation clearly.)
- self-righteousness (When we think we're always right ... an end-justifies-the-means attitude.)

Adapted from materials from the Josephson Institute of Ethics, josephsoninstitute.org.

Thomas Jefferson opposed slavery publicly, while all the while owning slaves.

26

> What you do speaks so loud that I cannot hear what you say.
> —Ralph Waldo Emerson

public. Ultimately, Nixon's lack of integrity cost him his presidency. He resigned rather than be *impeached*.

President Bill Clinton is another U.S. President who struggled with the issue of integrity. Clinton was a brilliant leader who led his country into one of its longest periods of peace and economic prosperity. Although he did not betray his country in the same way Nixon did, he did betray a moral standard when he engaged in sexual behaviors with a White House intern. Then, when the unsavory secret threatened to become public, he evaded the truth. Although many Americans felt that Clinton's personal problems had no bearing on his ability to lead the nation, ultimately his lack of personal integrity got in the way of accomplishing as much as he could of during his second term in office.

Politicians aren't the only ones who are judged by their reputations. Those around you will judge your character (including your integrity) based on these things:

- your clothes.
- your friends.
- how you talk.
- your grades.
- where you hang out.
- whether or not you smoke, do drugs, or drink.
- who you date.
- whether or not you break the law.
- how much money you have.
- how hard you work.

Which of these do you think are fair reasons for judging character? Which ones are not?

Long before either Nixon or Clinton faced their ethical dilemmas, Thomas Jefferson, one of America's earliest and greatest politicians, struggled with the same issue. Publicly, he opposed slavery; privately, he owned slaves. In fact, he had a secret relationship with a slave woman and was the father of at least one of her children—

and yet he never acknowledged her or admitted his responsibility to her. He *said* what he believed was right . . . and meanwhile, he *did* something he knew was wrong.

Jefferson wrote this about lying: "He who permits himself to tell a lie once finds it much easier to do a second and third time, till at length it becomes habitual; he lies without attending to it, and tells truths without the world's believing him. This falsehood of the tongue leads to that of the heart, and in time depraves all. . . ." Jefferson apparently knew about dishonesty firsthand; he may have been describing his own life.

Politicians are only human, of course, and everyone makes mistakes. But if you are going to be a public leader with integrity, then your public actions must not contradict your private life.

As Jefferson said, dishonesty is a habit, a hard one to break. Whatever career path you decide to travel, you'll find in the long run your way is smoother if you tell the truth. Don't wait. Make integrity a habit now.

I believe that truth is the glue that holds government together.
—Gerald Ford

Dr. Charles Koop, former Surgeon General, confers with Hillary Rodham Clinton.

RESPECT AND COMPASSION

If we truly have respect and compassion for others, then we will place others' needs ahead of our own ambitions.

CHAPTER THREE

D r. Charles Koop didn't set out to have a career in politics. Instead, he planned on demonstrating his compassion for others through his medical practice. He did, in fact, achieve this goal. From 1948 to 1981, he was the surgeon-in-chief at Philadelphia's Children's Hospital. There he had become a pioneer in *pediatric* surgery and created America's first *neonatal* intensive care nursery.

But in 1981, Dr. Koop's career took a sharp curve in a new direction. President Reagan appointed him Deputy Assistant Secretary for Health, and the following year Dr. Koop became Surgeon General.

Dr. Koop may have entered the world of politics—but he refused to abandon the principles of compassion and respect that had made him an outstanding doctor. Rather than keeping a low profile and courting the good opinion of the media, Dr. Koop was an outspoken advocate of public health issues.

For instance, he used his new political position to launch a campaign against smoking. Although the Public Health Service had been trying to call Americans' attention to tobacco's dangers, the Surgeons General before Koop had more or less evaded the issue. Koop was determined to spread the word that smoking can kill. His 1986 report on the dangers of *passive smoking* was an important milestone in the fight against smoking. He cared too much about people to keep silent.

Koop was also the first federal spokesperson on *AIDS*. Until Koop's report, Americans knew little about this new and deadly disease. Most of what they did know was rumors. To fight the superstition that was growing out of this ignorance, Koop wrote "Understanding AIDS," a Public Health Service brochure that was mailed

We owe much of our current understanding of the dangers of smoking to Dr. Koop.

Politicians have the power to influence the course of scientific research.

Those who show respect and compassion for others do so by:

- being courteous and polite.
- accepting those who are different from themselves.
- assisting those who are mistreated by others.
- sharing with others.
- doing what they can to help others in need.
- looking at a situation from the other's perspective.
- treating others as they would like to be treated.
- forgiving others.

Adapted from material from the Character Counts Coalition, charactercounts.org/overview/about.html

As Surgeon General, Dr. Koop was a member of the executive branch of the government, the branch that enforces the laws. In the United States, the executive branch includes these departments:

- Treasury
- Agriculture
- Energy
- Education
- Transportation
- Justice
- Heath and Human Services

In the United States, the President is the leader of the executive branch of government. In Canada, the Prime Minister has a similar role.

to 107 million households in 1988, the largest public health mailing ever. Koop made clear to the American public that AIDS was a health issue rather than a moral one; no one deserved this disease, and only education and research could fight it.

Not everyone appreciated Dr. Koop's approach to this and other issues. Koop, however, cared more about the well-being of others than he did

Many adolescents begin smoking despite Dr. Koop's warnings.

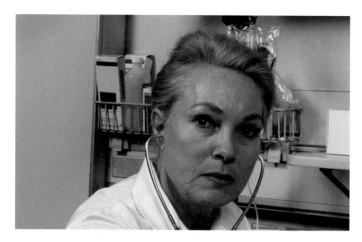

If you're outstanding in your field—no matter what that field is—you may one day succeed in politics as well.

about public opinion. His respect and compassion for human beings impelled him to speak out on many high-profile health issues. Eventually, he lost the political support of many of the people who had originally backed his appointment.

In October 1989, Koop resigned from his political position. He continued to educate the public about health issues through other

The position of Surgeon General was created in 1871. This person is appointed by the President of the United States (with the advice and consent of the Senate) for a four-year term of office. The Surgeon General reports to the Assistant Secretary for Health. He or she holds the rank of Vice Admiral in the U.S. Public Health Service Commissioned Corps, a uniformed military service. The minimum requirements for appointment as Surgeon General are:

- a medical degree from an accredited medical school;
- at least one year of postgraduate medical training;
- licensure to practice medicine in at least one of the 50 states.

means until his death in death in February, 2013. His good character came first, before power, prestige, or popularity.

Do you think you would have done the same in his place?

Career expert Richard Bolles believes that respect and compassion—or love—is an essential part of finding your ideal occupation. He writes:

Your unique and individual mission will most likely turn out to be a mission of Love, acted out in one or all of three arenas: either in the Kingdom of the Mind, whose goal is to bring more Truth into the world; or in the Kingdom of the Heart, whose goal is to bring more beauty into the world; or in the Kingdom of the Will, whose goal is to bring more Perfection into the world, through Service.

From *How to Find Your Mission in Life* by Richard Nelson Bolles (Berkeley, Calif.: Ten Speed Press, 2000), p. 58.

Maturity begins to grow when you can sense your concern for others outweighing your concern for yourself.

—John MacNaughton

Janet Reno demonstrated her commitment to justice in her role as U.S. Attorney General.

JUSTICE
AND FAIRNESS

*When you seek a just course of action,
not everyone will always agree
with your decisions.*

CHAPTER FOUR

Janet Reno was dedicated to justice. But as her political career progressed, she found that justice was not the simple, black-and-white concept she may once have imagined it to be.

Janet Reno knew what it was like to go against odds that were unfair. As one of only 16 women in her class of 500 at Harvard Law School, she knew that women were not treated the same as men in the legal world. When she graduated, she had a hard time finding work as a lawyer, simply because she was a woman.

Her strong sense of justice and fairness, however, inspired her to keep pushing her way upward through the legal system. In 1971,

Those who work in the nation's capital encounter both opportunities and challenges.

she was named staff director of the Judiciary Committee of the Florida House of Representatives, a position she used to help reform the Florida court system. In 1973 she accepted a position with the Dade County State's Attorney's Office. She left the state's attorney's office in 1976 to become a partner in a private law firm, but in 1978, Reno was appointed State Attorney General for Dade County. Next, she was elected to the Office of State Attorney in November 1978 and was reelected by the voters four more times. As always, she fought hard to see that everyone received the fair and just treatment they deserved. She helped reform the juvenile justice system, pursued delinquent fathers for child support payments, and established the Miami Drug Court.

In 1993, her hard work drew the attention of President Bill Clinton, and he appointed her as America's first woman Attorney General. Her priorities in this role were to:

- reduce crime and violence by incarcerating serious, repeat offenders and finding alternative forms of punishment for first time, nonviolent offenders.

People who value justice and fairness:

- treat all people the same (as much as possible).
- are open-minded; they are willing to listen to others' points of view and try to understand.
- consider carefully before making decisions that affect others.
- don't take advantage of others' mistakes.
- don't take more than their fair share.
- cooperate with others.
- recognize the uniqueness and value of each individual.

Adapted from material from the Character Counts Coalition, charactercounts.org/overview/about.html

- focus on prevention and early intervention efforts to keep children away from gangs, drugs, and violence, and on the road to strong, healthy and self-sufficient lives.
- enforce civil rights laws to ensure equal opportunity for all Americans.
- ensure that the Department of Justice reflects a diverse government, making integrity, excellence and professionalism the hallmarks of the Department.

Clearly justice was important to Reno.

Some, however, have accused Reno of being unjust and unfair, particularly in the circumstances surrounding Elian Gonzalez, a small boy from Cuba.

On November 22, 1999, Elian, his mother, and 12 other people from Cuba traveled toward the United States in a 16-foot motorboat. The boat capsized in rough seas; Elian was one of the only two survivors. After the Coast Guard rescued him, he was turned over to his great-uncle, who lived in Miami Beach.

The Attorney General is appointed by the President to be head of the Department of Justice and chief law enforcement officer of the federal government. He or she represents the United States in legal matters generally and gives advice and opinions to the President and to the heads of the executive departments of the government. The Attorney General appears in person to represent the government before the U.S. Supreme Court in cases that are unusually serious or important.

Elian's father, however, was still in Cuba, and he demanded that Elian be returned. Elian's uncle applied for asylum for the boy . . . and the story became increasingly complicated, drawing a great deal of media attention. Everyone had an opinion about what was the fair and just thing to do with Elian.

Janet Reno, however, was the person who had to make that decision. She met with Elian's father, and she agreed that Elian's place was with his father. Elian's relatives in Miami Beach refused to cooperate.

Janet Reno made a decision about what was the fair thing to do for Elian and his family.

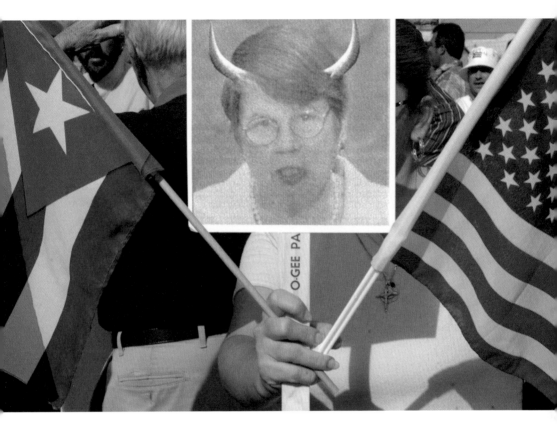

Doing what you believe is fair is not always the popular thing to do; many people were angry with Reno for the decision she made.

They would not allow Elian to go back to his father, despite a court order that commanded them to do so.

On April 22, 2000, after months of negotiation, Janet Reno felt that action had to be taken to enforce what she believed to be justice. She ordered armed federal agents to storm the Miami house. No one was hurt, but the television coverage of armed soldiers bursting through the door of Elian's uncle angered many Americans. Elian was flown out of Miami to Washington, where he was reunited with his father and allowed to return to Cuba. His relatives in Miami, as well as many others, were furious.

42

Janet Reno did what she believed to be the just and fair thing for both Elian and his father. Not everyone agreed with her views. As a political leader she had great power—but like all politicians, she was vulnerable to the changing tide of public opinion.

What would you have done in her place? Do you agree or disagree with the actions she took in regard to Elian Gonzalez?

A more important question is this: Do you possess a strong enough sense of justice that you would do what you believed to be fair—even if everyone disagreed with you?

For the sake of peace and justice, let us move toward a world in which all people are at least free to determine their own destiny.
                                                    —Ronald Reagan

In his presidential campaign, George Bush, Sr. was faced with decisions about his responsibilities to his party.

RESPONSIBILITY

*Ultimately, achieving success is not our
greatest responsibility in life.*

CHAPTER FIVE

Vice-President George Bush knew he had a responsibility to the Republican Party. The party had elected him as their candidate for the presidency. People were counting on him to win the election and lead the nation.

So in 1988, when his top campaign advisors told him that the latest Gallup poll showed he was 16 percentage points behind his Democratic rival, Michael Dukakis, Bush was worried. His advisors came up with a new strategy that would help turn the tide of public opinion in his favor. Bush decided to go with their idea.

The new advertising campaign used negative television ads to show Americans that Dukakis was soft on crime in his role as governor of Massachusetts. Again and again, Bush supporters told the story of Willie Horton, a convicted murderer who was allowed to leave the state on a weekend furlough program—and who then traveled to Maryland, where he assaulted a couple in their home. The Bush campaign arranged publicity tours for Horton's victims, and Vice-President Bush referred to Horton's story whenever he could. No one ever mentioned that every state in America had similar furlough programs for prisoners.

The Bush campaign used many television commercials that were based on half-truths or even out and out lies. George Bush, Sr. wanted to win—and he believed it was his responsibility to use whatever means he could to achieve his goal.

He wasn't the first politician to use negative means like these to gain popularity. In 1840, the supporters of William Harrison gossiped that his opponent, Martin Van Buren, wore women's corsets and used cologne. Theodore Roosevelt was said by his enemies to be a drunkard and a drug user. Franklin Roosevelt was whispered to be mentally ill. Nor was he the last politician. President Barack

Gossip that Martin Van Buren wore women's underwear may have hurt his presidential campaign.

Teddy Roosevelt's enemies spread rumors that he abused alcohol and drugs.

People who value responsibility:

- think before they act; they consider the possible consequences of their actions.
- accept responsibility for the consequences of their choices.
- don't blame others for their mistakes or take credit for others' achievements.
- don't make excuses.
- set a good example for others.
- pursue excellence in all they do.
- do the best with what they have.
- are dependable; others can rely on them.

Adapted from material from the Character Counts Coalition, charactercounts.org/overview/about.html

Franklin Roosevelt's opponents tried to hurt the popular president's reputation with rumors that he was mentally ill.

Responsible News Coverage vs. Sensationalism

The First Amendment to the U.S. Constitution guarantees the freedom of the press, and Canada has similar laws that guarantee the same freedom. This means that the government cannot *censor* what is printed in newspapers and magazines—or reported on the radio, television, or the Internet. Most Americans and Canadians agree that the media has an obligation to report the truth.

In recent years, however, news agencies have begun investigating the personal lives of many politicians. The media has tremendous political power. When it reports the personal scandals and wrongdoings of public officials, it has the power to destroy political careers. Political rivals can use this power to further their own ends.

Sensational news sells. People are fascinated by the latest scandal. But do news agencies have the right to report on the private lives of politicians—or should they respect the privacy of these people? What do you think?

One of politicians' biggest responsibilities is to keep on top of what's happening in the world. You can't lead others well if you don't know what's going on in their lives. Here are five ways you can begin developing this responsibility right now:

1. Read a newspaper every day.
2. Watch the Discovery Channel and news reports on television.
3. Discuss issues with others. Be sure to listen to their viewpoints and opinions.
4. Subscribe to a news magazine like *Newsweek* or *Time*.
5. Travel—and pay attention to the way others live in other parts of the country or world.

Obama has also been subject to negative rumors, such as when a small group of opponents claimed he was not an American citizen.

In the past, negative campaign strategies like these depended on rumor alone. Now, however, the media has become a powerful weapon that can be used against a political opponent. Political strategists study ways to slant news stories. Since big business owns many news agencies, alliances between politicians and business can further influence the stories we hear or read.

Some people believe that Dukakis lost his chance at the presidency because he refused to fight as dirty as Bush did. A few former Dukakis supporters have even said that by failing to fight back, Dukakis also failed to meet his responsibilities to his party.

What do you think? If you were to run for a political office, what would you consider your greatest responsibility to be?

And what would you have done if you had been in George Bush's place?

A Framework for Ethical Decision Making

Recognize a moral issue.
Ask yourself if there is something wrong, either personally or socially.
Are there conflicts in place which could damage people, animals, institutions, or society?

Go beyond concerns about legality.
Does this issue affect the dignity and rights of individuals?

Get the facts.
Investigate the relevant facts.
Decide which people have a stake in the outcome of this issue, and what that stake is.
Determine your options for acting.
Get the opinion of someone you respect about your list of options.
Make sure you have consulted all persons and groups involved.

Evaluate options from different moral perspectives.
Which option will do the most good, while doing the least harm?
Which option respects the rights and dignity of all stakeholders? Will each be treated fairly?
Which option best promotes the common good?
Which option encourages the development of the virtues and character traits we value?

Make a decision.
Considering all the questions above, which of the options is the right one?
Get the opinion of someone you respect on the option you've chosen.

Reflect afterward.
   Look back and determine how your decision turned out for everyone involved.
   Would you choose the same option if you had it to do over again?

Material adapted from the Markkula Center for Applied Ethics.

I am not bound to win, but I am bound to be true.
I am not bound to succeed, but I am bound to live up to what light I have.

—Abraham Lincoln

It takes courage to fight for your beliefs.

COURAGE

A lifetime spent doing the right thing, over and over, takes as much courage as a life of dramatic and daring deeds.

CHAPTER SIX

Growing up in Maine, young Deborah Simpson gave little thought to becoming a political leader. But the 1960s were a time of great political interest and action in the United States. Issues concerning the Vietnam War and movements to gain equal rights for all citizens were uppermost in the minds of many citizens. Deborah's parents had adopted strong political convictions, which they began to share with their young daughter. At the young age of ten, Deborah was already a volunteer for the McGovern campaign, trying to get democrat George McGovern elected as president in 1972.

Deborah Simpson is an example of a courageous politician.

People who value courage:

- say what's right (even when no one agrees with them).
- do the right thing (even when it's hard).
- follow their conscience instead of the crowd.
- are willing to take risks to accomplish what needs to be done.

Deborah's interest in political issues never waned, but she did not take a direct path to a political career. After high school, she entered the work force rather than going to college. She soon discovered that work options were limited because she lacked training and a degree. Caught in an abusive marriage, by the time she was in her 30s, she knew she needed to make some changes in her life.

Changing our lives is almost always frightening, even when the changes bring improvement. But Deborah gathered her courage and left her marriage. Even with a three-year-old child to support, Deborah realized she needed to return to school and obtain a degree. With a clear goal before her, Deborah had enough courageous determination to go to college part-time, work as a waitress, raise her son . . . and be an active political volunteer.

Becoming a teacher was the goal Deborah had set for herself, but two years before graduation, while she was working first on the reelection of a state senator and then on a *referendum*, other individuals engaged in these campaigns suggested that Deborah run for office. Even customers at the restaurant where she worked began to tell Deborah they thought she would be a good representative of the people.

Deborah was concerned about the impact of a political race on her son. After careful consideration, however, she determined that running for office was the right thing to do. She knew she was a

Since Simpson is herself a working mom, she understands the needs of working mothers in her constituency.

Practice Being Courageous and Allow Your Courage to Grow

From the time that we are very young, situations arise that provide opportunities for our courage to grow. A first step might be learning to sleep without a light on; later steps could include riding a school bus for the first time, providing answers to a teacher's questions in class, learning to ride a bike, getting a driver's license. Consider what you would do in the following courage-building situations.

You are on a school field trip with your classmates. After lunch, your waitress brings the bill to the table you are sharing with friends. You look over the bill and notice the waitress forgot to charge you for your lunch. You tell your friends that you need to inform the waitress of the oversight, but your friends say, "Don't be stupid. The restaurant will never notice, and you'll have extra money for afternoon activities." They all agree that the smart thing to do would be to keep the money. Would you:
1. keep quiet and enjoy the extra cash?
2. gather your courage, and explain to your friends that you could not enjoy the cash since it would be morally wrong to keep something that no longer belonged to you?

When you walk into the cafeteria with your new friend, you see a video lying on an empty table. You pick it up and find that it is already checked out of the library. Your friend decides to keep the video, and she invites you to spend the night at her house so you can watch it together. You've been wanting to spend the night at your friend's house ever since meeting her. Would you:
1. ask your parents if you could spend the night at the friend's house?
2. gather your courage—and offer to take the video back to the library and check it out?

Your drafting teacher gives your class an assignment to plan a kitchen. You enjoy the assignment so much that you add many extra touches like selecting color combinations and drawing a floor plan that includes placement of furniture. You're very pleased with your work when you hand in the assignment, but you are shocked to read the teacher's comments when you receive the assignment back. "I'm very impressed by this work," she explains, "so impressed that I realize you did not complete the assignment without help. Perhaps you based your kitchen on an existing room rather that drafting your own design." Would you:

1. be so embarassed that you remain quiet rather than telling the teacher that she is mistaken?
2. gather your courage, tell your parents what happened, tell your teacher that you are happy she was so impressed by your work, and then explain that you simply enjoyed the assignment so much you put a lot of extra thought into it?

You notice that your group of friends no longer invites Muhammad to participate in after-school activities. You suspect it might be because he is Muslim. Would you:

1. Just be glad you're included in the fun?
2. Gather your courage and ask them why they no longer include Muhammad. Remind them of what a good friend he has been, and that it's not fair to exclude him because of his religion.

strong person, and she had the courage to face unfair criticism; with her guidance, she was confident her son would be able to withstand it as well.

Shortly after this decision, Deborah was faced with an ethical dilemma. At that time, certain individuals were working on a referendum to repeal a law guaranteeing equal housing and employment rights; this law made it unlawful to discriminate against individuals because of sexual orientation. Another group working to protect the anti-discrimination law asked Deborah if they could insert their literature into the publicity packets she was distributing. Deborah was in favor of maintaining the equal-rights law, but she worried about losing votes in some parts of her district. She wondered how far she should go to stand up for her own beliefs. Would it be okay to stay quiet on this issue in order to be more assured of victory?

After much soul searching, Deborah made a courageous decision. She included the anti-discrimination materials in her campaign packet. She determined that she would always do the right thing, even if it meant losing an election, and she has never wavered from that commitment. And in 2000, Deborah L. Simpson won her election, becoming State Representative for a two-year term for District 73, which includes part of Auburn, Maine. She served as State Representative until 2008, when she became a State Senator until 2010.

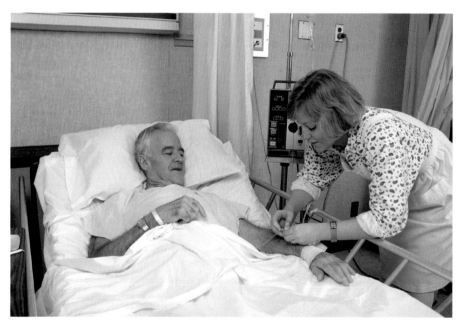

Politicians have the power to bring about improved medical care for everyone.

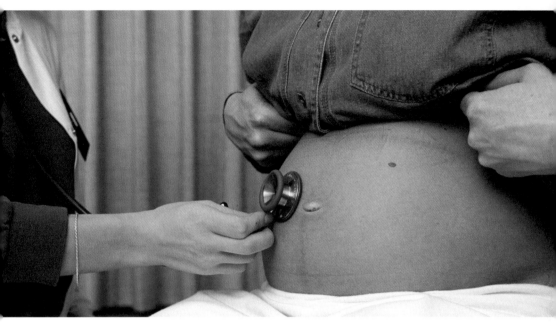

By improving health coverage for pregnant mothers, politicians influence future generations.

As a State Representative, Deborah's job was to draft laws and work on committees that conduct public hearings on laws drafted by other Representatives and State Senators; she also contributed to possible changes to current laws. In addition, Deborah solved problems brought to her attention by the people she represented.

Deborah faced another moral dilemma when the Maine governor introduced a bill to change the compensation law for injured workers. The bill would have saved much money for the state, and state representatives were pressured to support it. Deborah once again made a courageous commitment, however: she decided that she stands for injured workers, and she opposed the bill. She also worked to add mental health coverage to those receiving medical aid from the state.

When Deborah received a letter or a telephone call asking for assistance, she always was there to lend a helping hand. In 2001, a single mother told Deborah that her state income tax refund had been withheld for overpayment of public assistance. The woman was upset because she needed the money and puzzled because she had never been on welfare. Deborah investigated the situation and discovered the woman's mother had received the overpayment when this woman was only two years old. Deborah worked to get the woman's refund check to her and introduced a bill to prevent children from being held accountable for overpayments made to their parents. She has also introduced a bill to add breastfeeding to the human rights act. Now women in Maine cannot be prevented from feeding their babies in public places. Deborah has become a courageous leader who is not afraid to do whatever she believes is right.

She was also a tireless worker both for her constituents and for her family. Even though she often worked 65 or more hours per week as a legislator, because of the pay scale for state representatives in Maine, she had to supplement her family income. While some individuals might worry about "appearances" or be embarrassed to be seen in a more humble working situation, Deborah was not afraid to continue working as a waitress. After all, she was a servant of the people, and it gave her an opportunity to speak one-on-one with her constituents every Saturday night. She was a courageous politician—and for her, character came first.

Moral courage is a more rare commodity than bravery in battle.
—John F. Kennedy

Jimmy Carter's life demonstrates the qualities of self-discipline and diligence.

SELF-DISCIPLINE AND DILIGENCE

*Stay true to your goals—even
in the face of failure.*

CHAPTER SEVEN

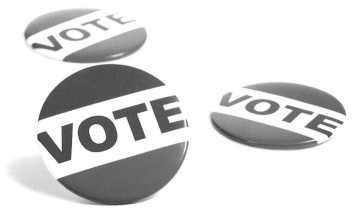

Jimmy Carter was always a self-disciplined and diligent man of principle. He was determined to do what he could to help his country. But at the time of his presidency, he was not considered to be a success.

Although Carter worked hard to fight his country's economic problems, the nation had fallen into a financial hole that was too deep for his efforts. By the end of his administration, the budget deficit had decreased, and eight million more people were employed—but interest rates and inflation were at all-time highs. His efforts to reduce them only caused a short *recession*, adding to his reputation as a poor president.

64

People who value self-discipline and diligence:

- work to control their emotions, words, actions, and impulses.
- give their best in all situations.
- keep going even when the going is rough.
- are determined and patient.
- try again even when they fail the first time.
- look for ways to do their work better.

Adapted from material from the Character Education Network.

The worst blow to his presidency, however, came from affairs outside the United States. In 1978, when the U.S. embassy staff in Iran were seized as hostages, many people felt America should go to war. Carter, however, was determined to find a peaceful resolution to the situation. He continued the long and difficult negotiations for the hostages' release, despite pressure to seek a more dramatic and militant solution. If America went to war, Carter knew that many innocent Iranians would be killed—and he was as determined to protect their lives as he was to save the captive Americans. His daring

Recycling is just one issue that politicians encounter in our world today.

Jimmy Carter and his wife Rosalind have worked hard for their country.

rescue attempt fell flat because of poor planning and failed equipment. In the end, on the same day he left office, Iran finally released the 52 hostages. This achievement came too late to save Carter's political career.

He had accomplished much during his years as President, however. For instance, he dealt with the energy shortage by establishing a national energy policy; he also prompted government efficiency through civil service reform. He improved the environment by expanding the national park system, including 103 million acres

"We must adjust to changing times and still hold to unchanging principles.... The work to which we have dedicated our lives is predicated on our simple belief that we share with our compatriots an enduring obligation to ensure and protect the human entitlements of life, liberty, and the pursuit of happiness both at home and abroad. We must always remember that America did not invent human rights ... human rights invented America."

From Jimmy Carter's speech upon winning the Presidential Medal of Freedom in 1999.

Although many people perceived Carter to be a weak president, he did not let political failure get in the way of his self-disciplined commitment to his ideals.

of Alaskan lands, and he created the Department of Education to increase human and social services. During his years as president, he appointed record numbers of women, African Americans, and Hispanic Americans to government jobs. Because of his efforts, the prime minister of Israel and Egypt's president sat down and agreed to a peace treaty. Carter never gave up trying to make America—and the entire world—a better place for everyone.

But all these accomplishments failed to capture the enthusiasm of the media. Although Carter was an intelligent man of character, most Americans saw him as a weak president who had failed to achieve much of anything.

Jimmy Carter possessed enough self-discipline, however, that he did

> The man who has done his level best . . . is a success, even though the world may write him down as a failure.
> —B.C. Forbes

Ways to Build Self-Discipline and Diligence

You don't have to wait to be an adult to practice this character trait. Here are some ideas for building it right now:

1. Use a planner for one month. When the month is over, evaluate whether you got more accomplished as a result of having a plan for each day or week. Decide whether you want to make the planner an ongoing part of your life.
2. Identify your biggest time-wasters (for example, television, the Internet, talking on the telephone). Resolve to cut at least one hour of time-wasting activity out of your life.
3. Think of something you've been putting off doing. Resolve to do it this week. Next week, do something else you've been procrastinating.
4. Evaluate how much influence peer pressure has on your life. Ask yourself, "Am I doing what I want to do (am I being self-disciplined)—or am I allowing someone else to make my decisions for me?"

Adapted from *The 7 Habits of Highly Effective Teens* by Sean Covey (New York: Simon & Schuster, 1998), p. 128.

Jimmy Carter works with Habitat for Humanity so that needy people can have their own homes.

"Can-Do" vs. "No-Can-Do"

Politicians who want to change the world have to be "can-do" people.

Can-Do People
Make things happen.
Think about solutions
  and options.
Act.

No-Can-Do People
Wait for things to happen.
Think about problems and barriers.

Sit back and watch while others act.

Which kind of person are you?

Never despair, but if you do, work on in despair.
—Edmund Burke

not let political failure destroy his diligence. After he left office, he continued to work for the ideals in which he believed. He wrote book after book (27 in all), and he founded the Carter Center, which works to resolve conflicts, promote

Author Jay McGraw believes that self-discipline and diligence are necessary character traits for success. When we put these character traits into practice...

* we will encounter problems, but there will be nothing we can't manage.
* we can learn to be the managers of our own lives.
* we can make life management a priority.
* we develop a goal plan—and be successful.

Adapted from *Life Strategies for Teens* by Jay McGraw (New York: Simon & Schuster, 2000), p. 173.

Habitat for Humanity works to rebuild and renovate buildings like this one, providing homes for those who could not other-wise afford them.

democracy, protect human rights, and prevent diseases around the world; it also advances health and agriculture in developing nations. He and his wife are regular volunteers for Habitat for Humanity, a nonprofit organization that helps needy people renovate and build homes for themselves.

Jimmy Carter has still not given up. His determination and diligence have won him the respect of many who once criticized him as a president.

When you experience failure, are you tempted to abandon your original goals? What can you learn from Jimmy Carter's example?

Press on. Nothing in the world can take the place of persistence.
—Ray A. Kroc

Those who serve in their nation's capital have the opportunity to create a better community for everyone.

CITIZENSHIP

When you put the other character traits to work for the good of your community, you become a powerful citizen.

CHAPTER EIGHT

Gaylord Nelson loved nature. As a politician he did not use his position to simply advance his own power and prestige; instead, he believed the government should serve the human community—and protect their world, the Earth.

Nelson grew up in a tiny town in northwest Wisconsin. There he learned his views on citizenship and nature. "It was the kind of community where everyone knew everyone else," Nelson said years later, "where everyone was concerned about everyone else." He also recalled, "There was never any reason to believe that the rest of the world wasn't as clean and comfortable as northern Wisconsin. It was easy for the children [in Wisconsin] to believe that the legacy

Members of the U.S. Congress create laws that guard the safety of communities, conserve natural resources, and protect the environment.

they had inherited in rich land, clean air, and safe water was one that every boy and girl in the nation had."

As a boy, Nelson loved to listen to the adults discussing politics around the dinner table. His family had a history of public service: his father had served as mayor of their town, and his mother was a member of several important political committees. They had passionate opinions about the government, and their enthusiasm inspired their son to set his sights on becoming a politician. He feared, though, that by the time he grew up, the country's leaders would have already solved all the nation's problems, leaving none left for him to tackle.

As he grew older, however, he realized that unfortunately the world was full of an endless supply of problems. He was eager to do what he could to help. At 14, he got his first taste of politics when he tried to persuade the town council to plant elm trees along the five roads that led into his town. The council refused, and Nelson learned an important lesson: losing is a part of politics—and self-discipline and diligence in the face of failure is what makes powerful citizenship possible. He did not give up but continued to seek ways to serve his community through politics.

Nelson eventually earned a law degree and then served four years in the Army during World War II. Afterward, he ran for a seat in Wisconsin's state assembly—and lost. Two years later, he ran again. This time, he won. He held the senate seat for the next ten years.

Nelson used his political position to gain power as a leader. However, he did not use that power selfishly but instead considered it to be a tool for influencing the issues that concerned him. At the top of his list were education and conservation. Nelson was still doing all he could to solve his community's problems. Most of all, he wanted to protect the environment for future generations.

When Nelson became governor of Wisconsin in 1958, he stayed true to his ideals. He began a ten-year $50 million program to buy private lands and preserve them as wilderness areas. Under his leadership, Wisconsin became a pioneer in environmental protection.

According to the Character Counts Coalition, citizenship is:

- playing by the rules.
- obeying the law.
- doing your share.
- respecting authority.
- keeping informed about current events.
- voting.
- protecting your neighbors and community.
- paying your taxes.
- giving to others in your community who are in need.
- volunteering to help.
- protecting the environment.
- conserving natural resources for the future.

The first Earth Day included:

- 2,000 colleges;
- over 10,000 private and public schools;
- over 20 million Americans.

Earth Day continues to be an annual event across America.

Senator Nelson's citizenship helped bring about these important parts of today's conservation effort:

- Environmental Protection Agency
- National Pesticide Control Act
- Water Quality Act
- Clean Air Act
- National Lakes Preservation Act
- Wild Rivers Act
- National Hiking Trails System

After two terms as governor, Nelson was elected as a U.S. senator in 1962. He planned to use his new position to push the federal government toward becoming involved in environmental issues. The problems facing the nation's natural resources, he believed, were too big for the states to tackle on their own. "We cannot be blind," he said in his first speech on the Senate floor, "to the growing crisis of our environment. Our soil, our water, and our air are becoming more polluted every day. Our most priceless natural resources—trees, lakes, rivers, wildlife habitats—are being destroyed."

Garbage is one of the modern world's problems.

Senator Nelson helped begin the recycling movement.

In the 1960s, very few politicians were talking about environmental issues. But Nelson had enough courageous citizenship to change all that. His personal integrity, his respect and compassion for all citizens, and his sense of responsibility to future generations all helped him use his political position for the benefit of his community. In his 18 years as senator, he worked hard to make sure new laws were passed to protect the Earth.

He did not win all his battles—but he never gave up. "We must continue to fight the destruction of our natural environment," he wrote. Nelson realized that he could not bring about new laws until people's attitudes changed. He decided to call for a national "teach-in" to educate Americans on the environment's crisis.

On April 22, 1970, because of Senator Nelson, communities across the United States took part in Earth Day activities. Each community celebrated the event in its own way.

- In Manhattan, over 100,000 people walked in a nonpolluting parade.
- West Virginia students picked up five tons of trash along a short stretch of highway and dumped it on the steps of the county courthouse.

Ways to Contribute to Your Community

1. Recycle.
2. Find out what your local homeless shelter or mission needs; organize a community drive to collect food, clothing, etc., to fill that need.
3. Volunteer to read to senior citizens at a local retirement center.
4. Volunteer to help senior citizens do crafts at a local retirement-center.
5. Volunteer to teach senior citizens to use a computer.
6. Volunteer to walk a senior citizen's pet.
7. Plant trees.
8. Volunteer for a literacy program, to teach someone to read.
9. Help feed the hungry on holidays.
10. Volunteer for Meals On Wheels.

Adapted from *The Kid's Guide to Service Projects: Over 500 Service Ideas for Young People Who Want to Make a Difference*, by Barbara A. Lewis

- Girl Scouts in Washington, D.C., used canoes to dredge out piles of junk from the Potomac River.
- High school students in Omaha, Nebraska, made a tin mountain out of the more than 156,000 beer and soda cans they collected.

Some Americans wore gas masks to protest air pollution. Others elected "the biggest polluter" in their community. Nearly every community found a way to spread the word that protecting our Earth is important.

Meanwhile, Nelson spent the day making speeches across America. He asked his listeners to consider themselves not only citizens of the United States but citizens of the Earth. He called this concept "environmental citizenship." Tougher, environmental protection laws were one concrete result of all his efforts.

Earth Day events often include collecting enormous piles of glass or aluminum.

Despite his successes, however, his political career eventually came to an end when he ran for his fourth Senate term in 1980. After this loss, he went to work for the Wilderness Society. There he continued to work to keep politicians informed about the environment. He said: "It is time for our political leaders to recognize this truth: the fate of the living planet is the most important issue facing mankind."

Gaylord Nelson cared enough to make a difference in his community. Do you?

Ask not what your country can do for you, ask what you can do for your country.

—John F. Kennedy

Politicians' opportunities range from small-town politics to the national arena.

CAREER OPPORTUNITIES

Politicians have opportunities for power and prestige—and the chance to do good.

CHAPTER NINE

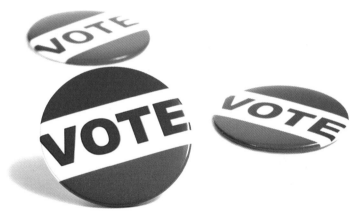

L inda Lewis wanted to make a difference to her community. She had gained a public reputation by working on several volunteer committees, and now she ran for a position on the school board. After her election, she worked hard for several years, doing all she could to make the community's school a safe, stimulating, and happy place. Linda had more ideas, though, both for the school and for the rest of the community, and she wanted the opportunity to work full time for her town. Eventually she decided to run for mayor. After a long and strenuous campaign, she was elected—and now she continues to work to bring about positive change for the people in her town.

84

Linda's experience may seem light years away from Abraham Lincoln's or some of the other politicians' we've discussed in this book. Being mayor of a small town and being President of the United States are at opposite ends of the political spectrum—and yet both mayor and President are politicians, elected by voters to be government leaders.

As citizens we often forget how much our government does for us—and yet there are few areas of our lives that are not touched in some way by the government. The federal government defends us from foreign aggression, enforces laws, and administers many different programs and agencies. Whenever we watch a weather forecast; each time we buy fresh, healthy food at the grocery store; when we travel by highway or air; and every time we make a deposit or withdraw funds from a bank account, we have the federal government to thank. At the state and local levels as well, governments provide vital community services—like public safety, healthcare, education, utilities, and courts. Government efforts improve our lives in countless ways every day.

If you decide to pursue a career in politics, you will have a chance to participate in this vital force that surrounds us all. Politi-

Across North America, politicians have the opportunity to serve their nations.

A politician of character must be able to handle the power and prestige that come with the job.

Politicians encounter varying opportunities for financial gain, depending on their level in government.

cal leaders have the chance to shape policies, build new programs, and improve old systems. Politicians both lead and serve their communities. They have the opportunity to make life better for us all.

Politicians have other opportunities as well, of course, opportunities that involve power and prestige. Whether mayor of a small town or Prime Minister or President of a nation, politicians are well-known and respected figures in their communities. They usually have great power within that community (whether the community is a village or a nation).

The opportunity for financial gain, however, varies a great deal for politicians. Effective January 2001, the President of the United States makes $400,000 a year and the Vice President makes $192,600. A mayor of a small town, however, may make less than $10,000 a year. Politicians' pay ranges somewhere between these two extremes. For instance, the salary for members of Congress (as of December 2012) is $150,000 a year; the average salary for a county executive is $71,000.

Job openings for the future are difficult to predict. At the federal level, the factors that affect openings are unique. In the United States,

Politicians have opportunities to confront issues and bring about change. Here are some of the important issues in our world today:

- environmental conservation
- the development of new energy sources
- abortion
- education
- Welfare reform
- gun control
- campaign finance practices
- national security
- pollution
- tax reform
- diversity and tolerance
- women's concerns
- child protection
- free speech (particularly as it relates to the Internet)
- homelessness
- drug law enforcement/legalization

Do you feel passionate about any of these issues? Do you care enough to want to get involved at the political level to bring about change?

Congress and the President determine the government's payroll budget each year. Each presidential administration and Congress has different public policy priorities, and this results in increases in levels of openings in some areas—and decreases in others. There will probably be about the same number of political jobs in the future, at least through 2018. There may be some jobs added as a result of a couple of factors: increasing population and states' and local governments' increasing responsibilities for services once provided by the federal government. However, as federal budget aid is decreased, citizens

Character cannot be summoned at the moment of crisis if it has been squandered by many years of compromise and rationalization. The only testing ground for the heroic is the mundane. The only preparation for that one profound decision which can change a life is those hundreds of self-defining seemingly insignificant decisions made in private. Habit is the daily battleground of character.
—Senator Dan Coats

will have to assume the costs through tax increases—and some communities may be resistant to this. As a result, in some communities, government positions may be cut back.

Advancement is an important opportunity for politicians. These opportunities usually progress in steps within a particular jurisdiction. For example, a local council member may run for mayor or for a position in state government; state legislators may decide to run for Congress or governor; governors or members of Congress may one day decide to run for President.

A politician leads the way in the race toward the future; since others will follow, he needs to never lose sight of the core qualities of a good character.

Canadian vs. American Government

Canada and the United States are both **democracies**, and they each have a written constitution whose meaning is interpreted by the courts—but the two governments also have important differences.

- In the United States the President is both the head of state and the head of the government. In Canada, the British Queen is the head of state, while the Prime Minister is the head of government.
- American government is based on the separation (and balance) of powers; the President cannot be a member of Congress. Canada's parliamentary government is based on a concentration of powers; the Prime Minister is also a member of either the House of Commons or the Senate.
- American officials are elected for a fixed term. (For example, a President can only serve for four years without a new election, and a President can serve at most for two terms.) Canadian officials are not elected for a fixed term; if the Government and the House of Commons are locked in disagreement, then a new election is called within two or three months.
- American government depends on the Constitution to spell out the duties and privileges of elected officials. Canada's government depends more on tradition and convention than on written regulations.
- In the United States, certain rights are maintained by the state and local governments. In Canada, the federal government is stronger and more centralized.

As you can see, the opportunities to be found in a political career are somewhat unique from other careers, and predictions about the future are dependent on complicated and interwoven factors. The fact remains, however, that our communities will always need leaders.

What Are Your Values?

Ask yourself these questions:

- What do I believe in?
- What is most important to me?
- What do I stand for?
- What gives my life meaning?
- What controls my actions?
- What goals do I want to reach?

As one of those leaders, perhaps the most important opportunity a politician faces is the chance to do good in his or her community. Each day of their professional lives, politicians have the chance to:

- demonstrate integrity and trustworthiness.
- treat others with respect and compassion.
- show justice and fairness.
- act responsibly.
- face challenges with courage.
- be self-disciplined and diligent enough to keep trying and never give up.
- make a difference in their communities through practicing good citizenship.

Practicing these core qualities of a good character does not come automatically, though. Because of their power, politicians also have plenty of opportunities for corruption and immoral actions. As individuals, they must all make the choice: which opportunities will they choose and which will they reject? Will they choose to do good—or will they choose to hurt others with their power?

In one way or another, all of us face that same choice.

Let us be shy no longer. Let us go to our strength. Let us offer hope. Let us tell the world that a new age is not only possible but probable.
—Ronald Reagan

Further Reading

Baxter, Neale. *Opportunities in State and Local Government Careers.* New York: McGraw-Hill, 2001.

Bike, William S. *Winning Political Campaigns.* Juneau, Alaska: Denali, 2001.

Covey, Sean. *The 7 Habits of Highly Effective Teens.* New York: Simon & Schuster, 2012.

McNamara, Michael. *The Political Campaign Desk Reference.* Parker, Col.: Outskirts Press, 2012.

Josephson, Michael S. and Wes Hanson, editors. *The Power of Character.* Bloomington, Ind.: Unlimited Press, 2004.

Kidder, Rushworth M. *How Good People Make Tough Choices.* New York: HarperCollins, 2009.

McGraw, Jay. *Life Strategies for Teens.* New York: Simon & Schuster, 2000.

Rowh, Mark. *Great Jobs for Political Science Majors.* New York: McGraw-Hill, 2004.

For More Information

Center for the 4th and 5th Rs (information on character issues)
www.cortland.edu/c4n5rs

Character Education Network
www.charactered.net

FirstGov (information about politics and Washington)
firstgov.gov

Josephson Institute of Ethics
www.josephsoninstitute.org

Young Politicians of America
www.ypa.org

Publisher's Note:
The websites on this page were active at the time of publication. The publisher is not responsible for websites that have changed their address or discontinued operation since the date of publication. The publisher will review and update the websites upon each reprint.

Glossary

AIDS   Acquired immunodeficiency syndrome, a disease of the human immune system transmitted by blood and bodily secretions.

Campaigns   A connected series of actions designed to bring about a desired goal (for instance, an election).

Censor   To examine in order to delete or remove anything that might be harmful to a particular viewpoint or power.

Charisma   A personal leadership magic that attracts the loyalty of others.

Circuits   Courts that sit at two or more places within a judicial district.

Confederacy   The eleven Southern states that dropped out of the Union in 1860 and 1861.

Democracies   Systems of government where people hold the power, either directly or indirectly through a system or representation and free elections.

Impeached   Charged with official misconduct while in office.

Media   Means of mass communication, such as newspapers, magazines, radio, and television.

Neonatal   Newborn.

Passive smoking   The smoke inhaled by nonsmokers when they are around people who are smoking.

Pediatric   Having to do with medical treatments for children.

Ratified Formally approved and invested with legal authority.

Recession   A period of reduced economic activity.

Referendum   A direct vote by citizens on a particular issue.

Savvy   Practical know-how.

Index

About the Author & Consultants

Ellyn Sanna has authored more than 50 books, including adult non-fiction, novels, young adult biographies, and gift books.

Cheryl Gholar is a Community and Economic Development Educator with the University of Illinois Extension. She has a Ph.D. in Educational Leadership and Policy Studies from Loyola University, and she has more than 20 years of experience with the Chicago Public Schools as a teacher, counselor, guidance coordinator, and administrator. Recognized for her expertise in the field of character education, Dr. Gholar assisted in developing the K–12 Character Education Curriculum for the Chicago Public Schools, and she is a five-year participant in the White House Conference on Character Building for a Democratic and Civil Society. The recipient of numerous awards, she is also the author of *Beyond Rhetoric and Rainbows: A Journey to the Place Where Learning Lives.*

Ernestine G. Riggs is an Assistant Professor at Loyola University Chicago and a Senior Program Consultant for the North Central Regional Educational Laboratory. She has a Ph.D. in Educational Leadership and Policy Studies from Loyola University, and she has been involved in the field of education for more than 35 years. An advocate of teaching the whole child, she is a frequent presenter at district and national conferences; she also serves as a consultant for several state boards of education. Dr. Riggs has received many citations, including an award from the United States Department of Defense Overseas Schools for Outstanding Elementary Teacher of America.